TAYLOR SWIFT

LYRIC TRIVIA

HANNAH KURRY

THIS IS A STATE OF GRACE. THIS IS THE WORTHWHILE FIGHT

____

_______________________ *(write your answer)*

____

____

I REMEMBER HOW WE FELT SITTING BY THE WATER

____

____

____

____

YOU NEVER HAVE TO SAY THAT YOU WERE WRONG.

____

____

State of Grace
Stay Stay Stay
Mine
Fortnight

I DIDN'T OPT IN TO BE YOUR ODD MAN OUT

(write your answer)

YOU LOW-DOWN BOY, YOU STAND-UP GUY

IT'S BLUE, THE FEELING I'VE GOT

I WAS GRINNIN' LIKE I'M WINNIN'

WILL YOU CALL WHEN YOU'RE BACK AT SCHOOL?

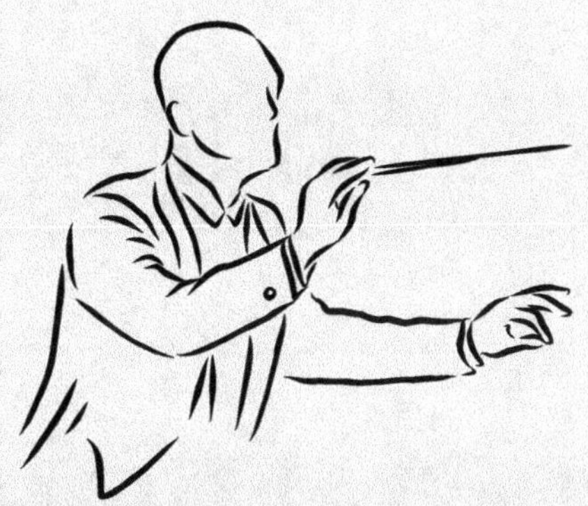

So Long, London
lol
Cruel Summer
I Can Do It With a Broken Heart
august

YOU DIDN'T MEASURE UP IN ANY MEASURE OF A MAN

____

_______________________ *(write your answer)*

____

____

HE SENT ME "DOWNTOWN LIGHTS"... I HADN'T HEARD IT IN A WHILE

HONEY, I ROSE UP FROM THE DEAD, I DO IT ALL THE TIME

____

____

____

____

ARE YOU GONNA MARRY, KISS, OR KILL ME?

I'LL STARE DIRECTLY AT THE SUN

____

____

The Smallest Man Who Ever Lived
Guilty as Sin
Look What You Made Me Do
So High School
Anti-Hero

IN THE GARDEN, WOULD YOU TRUST ME

____
____
(write your answer)

____
____

I LEAP FROM THE GALLOWS AND I LEVITATE DOWN YOUR STREET

BUT YOU'LL COME BACK EACH TIME YOU LEAVE

____
____

____
____

HE CAN'T KEEP HIS WILD EYES ON THE ROAD

REMEMBER LOOKIN' AT THIS ROOM?

____
____

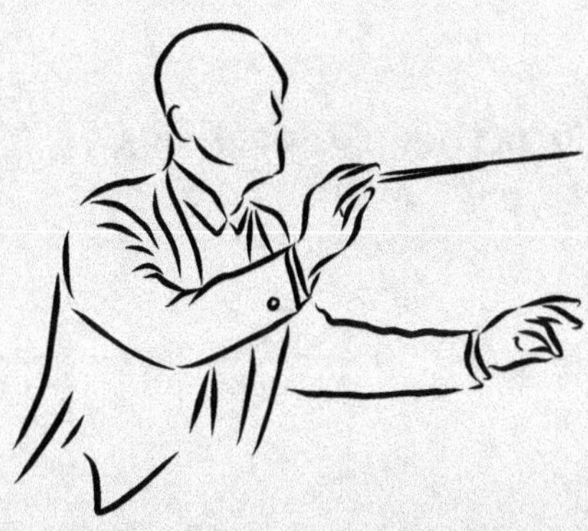

betty
Who's Afraid of Little Old Me
Blank Space
Style
You're Losing Me (From The Vault)

NO ONE HAS TO KNOW

____

_______________________ *(write your answer)*

____

IS THAT A BAD THING TO SAY IN A SONG?

YOU LIKE THE BAD ONES TOO

____

____

I'M BEGGING FOR YOU TO TAKE MY HAND

YOU JUST NEED TO TAKE SEVERAL SEATS AND THEN TRY TO RESTORE THE PEACE

____

____

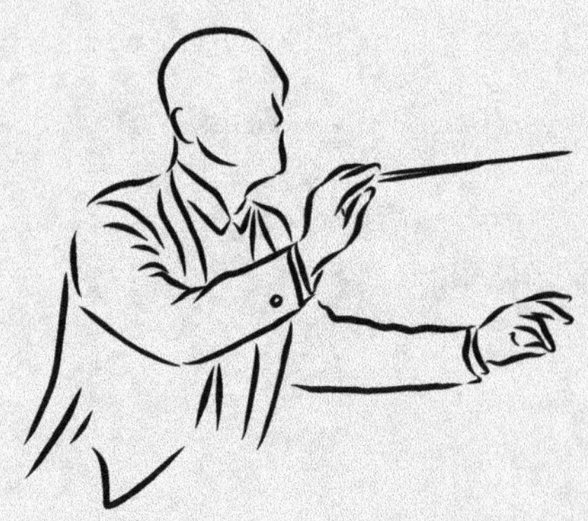

You Need To Calm Down
willow
End Game
Florida!!!
...Ready for It?

I LEFT MY SCARF THERE AT YOUR SISTER'S HOUSE

____

____

(write your answer)

____

____

EVERYTHING COMES OUT TEENAGE PETULANCE

WHAT A GHOSTLY SCENE

____

____

____

____

EVERYTHING YOU LOSE IS A STEP YOU TAKE

IT'S GONNA BE ALRIGHT, I DID MY TIME

____

____

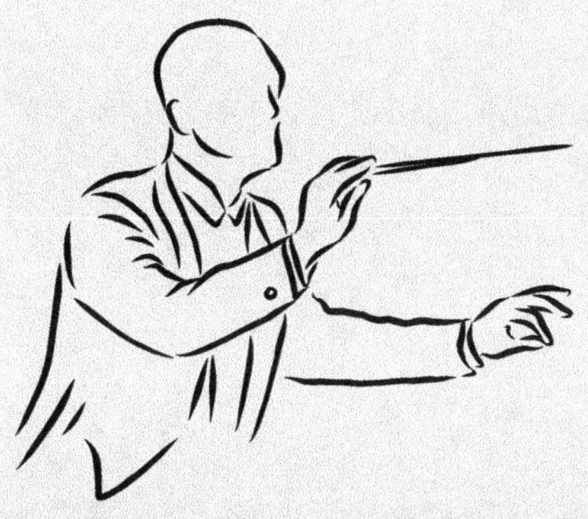

All Too Well
Down Bad
my tears ricochet
You're On Your Own, Kid
Fresh Out The Slammer

DON'T BE AFRAID,
WE'LL MAKE IT OUT
OF THIS MESS

____

____

(write your answer)

____

____

HOW THE HELL DID
WE LOSE SIGHT OF
US AGAIN?

ASK ME WHY SO
MANY FADE, BUT
I'M STILL HERE

____

____

____

____

LOVE YOU TO THE
MOON AND TO
SATURN

FIFTY YEARS IS A
LONG TIME

____

____

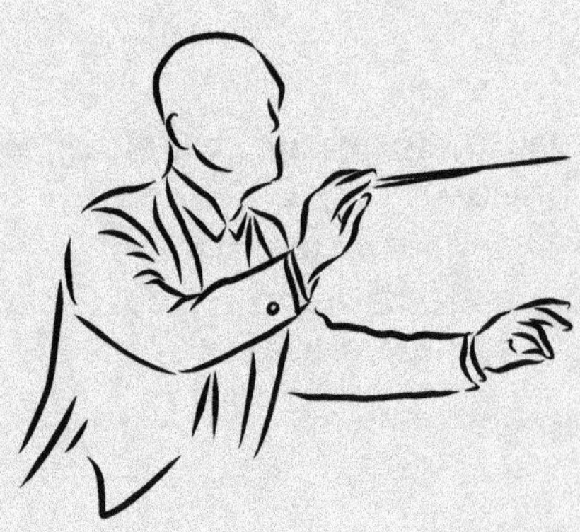

Love Story
Maroon
Karma
seven
the last great american dynasty

YOU'RE A FLASHBACK
IN A FILM REEL ON
THE ONE SCREEN IN
MY TOWN

____

_______________________ *(write your answer)*

____

____

YOU MUST LIKE ME
FOR ME

I SEE THIS FOR WHAT
IT IS

____

____

____

____

YOU TAUGHT ME A
SECRET LANGUAGE I
CAN'T SPEAK WITH
ANYONE ELSE

I WANT TO WEAR HIS
INITIAL ON A CHAIN
'ROUND MY NECK

____

____

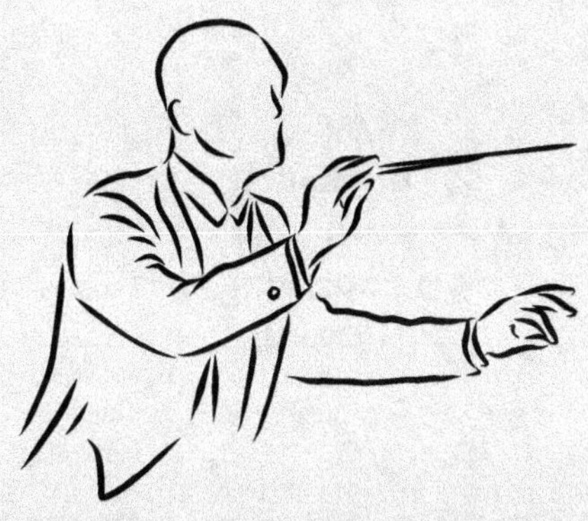

this is me trying
Delicate
happiness
illicit affairs
Call it What You Want

I GO ON TOO MANY DATES

____

____
(write your answer)

____

____

WHY'D YOU HAVE TO LEAD ME ON? WHY'D YOU HAVE TO TWIST THE KNIFE?

HE HAD A HALO OF THE HIGHEST GRADE HE JUST HADN'T MET ME YET

____

____

____

____

DID YOU LEAVE HER HOUSE IN THE MIDDLE OF THE NIGHT?

MY PAIN FITS IN THE PALM OF YOUR FREEZING HAND

____

____

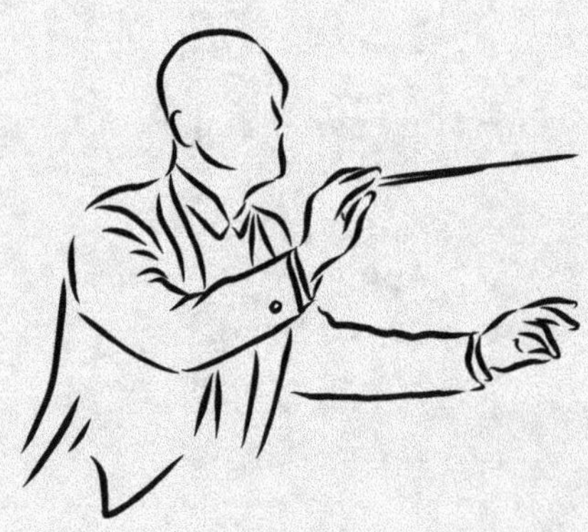

Shake It Off
Say Don't Go
I Can Fix Him (No Really I Can)
Question...?
ivy

I MOVE THROUGH THE
WORLD WITH THE
HEARTBROKEN

____

____

(write your answer)

WE WERE BORN TO
BE THE PAWN
IN EVERY LOVER'S
GAME

____

____

QUICK, QUICK, TELL
ME SOMETHING
AWFUL

____

____

I'VE NEVER SEEN
SOMEONE LIT FROM
WITHIN

THEY CALLED OFF THE
CIRCUS, BURNED THE
DISCO DOWN

____

____

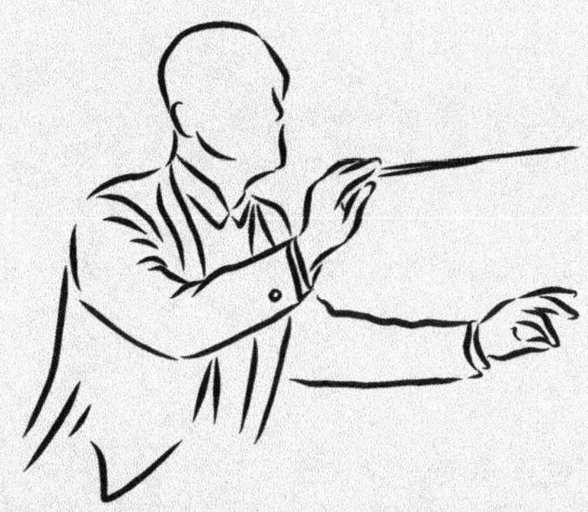

The Black Dog
Mastermind
I Hate It Here
Snow On The Beach
mirrorball

I REPLAY MY
FOOTSTEPS ON EACH
STEPPING STONE

____
____

____
____

AND THE GOD'S
HONEST TRUTH IS
THAT THE PAIN WAS
HEAVEN

OH, IT'S SO SAD TO
THINK ABOUT THE
GOOD TIMES

____
____

____
____

YOU SHOULD TAKE
IT AS A COMPLIMENT
THAT I'M TALKIN' TO
EVERYONE HERE BUT
YOU

HE POISONED THE
WELL, I WAS LYIN' TO
MYSELF

____
____

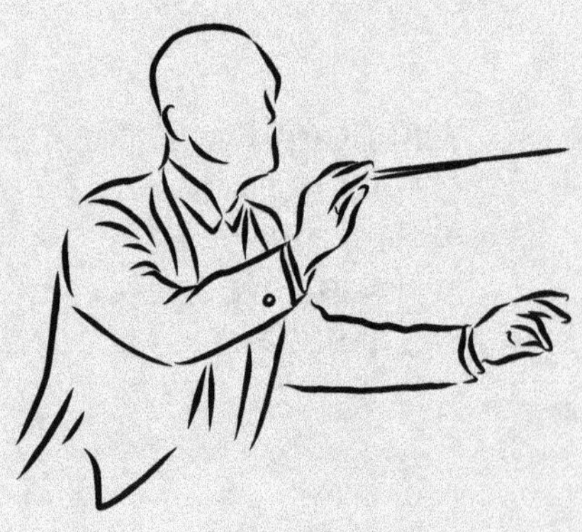

evermore
Would've, Could've, Should've
Bad Blood
Gorgeous
Getaway Car

ALL THE LOVE WE
UNRAVEL
AND THE LIFE I GAVE
AWAY

____

____
(write your answer)

____

____

THERE'S ROBBERS TO
THE EAST, CLOWNS
TO THE WEST

THE STORY ISN'T MINE
ANYMORE

____

____

____

____

I DON'T LIKE THAT
FALLING FEELS LIKE
FLYING 'TIL THE BONE
CRUSH

SHE DOESN'T GET
YOUR HUMOR LIKE I
DO

____

____

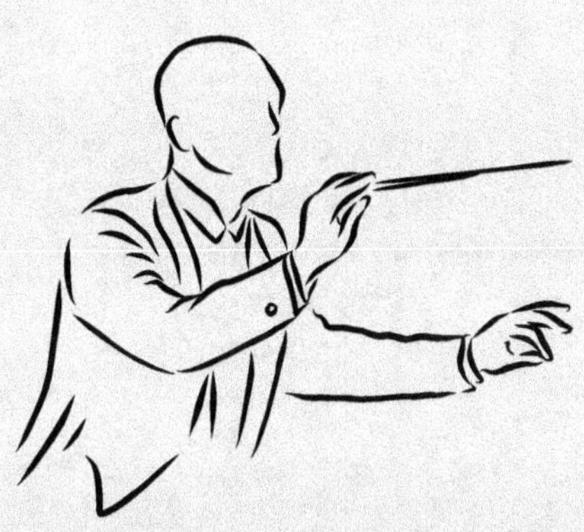

Midnight Rain
peace
The Manuscript
gold rush
You Belong With Me

I ONCE WAS POISON IVY, BUT NOW, I'M YOUR DAISY

____

_______________________ *(write your answer)*

____

____

I WOUNDED THE GOOD AND I TRUSTED THE WICKED

I JUST WANNA KEEP CALLING YOUR NAME

____

____

____

____

I NEVER GREW UP, IT'S GETTING SO OLD

THEY'D SAY I HUSTLED, PUT IN THE WORK

____

____

Don't Blame Me
Daylight
I Don't Wanna Live Forever
The Archer
The Man

THE EMPATHETIC HUNGER DESCENDS

____

____

(write your answer)

____

____

ALL OF THIS SILENCE AND PATIENCE, PINING AND ANTICIPATION

____

____

____

____

THE ONLY KINDA GIRL THEY SEE IS A ONE-NIGHT OR A WIFE

____

____

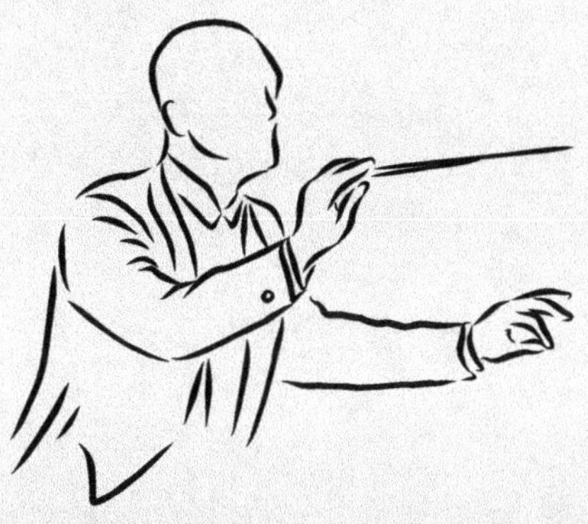

How Did it End?
Chloe or Sam or Sophia or Marcus
Dress
The Prophecy
Lavender Haze

YOU'LL POKE THAT
BEAR 'TIL HER CLAWS
COME OUT

____

____

DON'T WANT NO
OTHER SHADE OF
BLUE BUT YOU

SAY YOU'LL
REMEMBER ME
STANDIN' IN A NICE
DRESS

____

____

I THOUGHT IT WAS
JUST GOODBYE FOR
NOW

NO, THERE AIN'T NO
DOUBT
SOMEBODY'S GOTTA
CATCH HIM OUT

____

____

mad woman
hoax
Wildest Dreams
Peter no body,
no crime

IF HE DROPS MY NAME, THEN I OWE HIM NOTHIN'

____

____

(write your answer)

____

____

SOMEONE'S MOTHER HOLDS YOUR HAND THROUGH PLASTIC NOW

WE'RE SO SAD, WE PAINT THE TOWN BLUE

____

____

____

____

I WANT THE PENTHOUSE OF YOUR HEART

WHAT WOULD YOU DO IF WE NEVER MADE A SOUND?

____

____

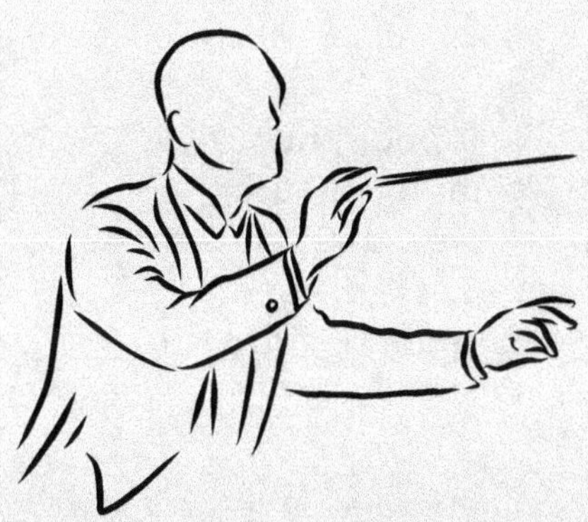

I Did Something Bad
epiphany
Miss Americana & The Heartbreak Prince
Bejeweled
I Can See You

BUT I'M GONNA GET YOU BACK

____

(write your answer)

____

THOSE WINDERMERE PEAKS LOOK LIKE A PERFECT PLACE TO CRY

WE'RE SO SAD, WE PAINT THE TOWN BLUE

____

____

I WONDER 'TIL I'M WIDE AWAKE

I HOPE I NEVER LOSE YOU, DID YOU HAVE TO RUIN WHAT WAS SHINY?

____

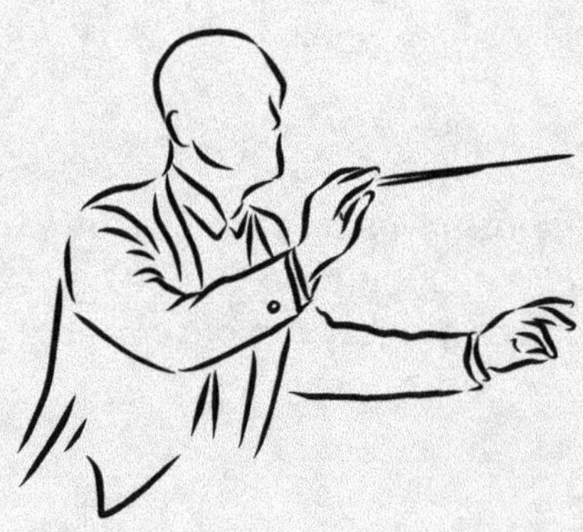

imgonnagetyouback
the lakes
Enchanted
Cornelia Street
Bad Blood

THEY FILLED MY CELL
WITH SNAKES, I
REGRET TO SAY

____

____

(write your answer)

THERE'S AN ACHE IN
YOU, PUT THERE BY
THE ACHE IN ME

EVERY DEAD-END
STREET LED YOU
STRAIGHT TO ME

SOMETHIN'
HAPPENED, I HEARD
HIM LAUGHIN'

THAT WAS ALL
BEFORE I LOCKED
IT DOWN

cowboy like me
London Boy
All Of The Girls You Loved Before
'tis the damn season
Cassandra

THAT YOU EVER WANTED FROM ME WAS NOTHIN'

____

____

(write your answer)

____

____

I'M NEVER GONNA MEET WHAT SHOULD'VE BEEN YOU

THE ONLY THING WE SHARE IS THIS SMALL TOWN

____

____

____

____

I'M THE ONE WHO BURNED US DOWN

SALUTE TO ME, I'M YOUR AMERICAN QUEEN

____

____

"ONE LESS TEMPTRESS, ONE LESS DAGGER TO SHARPEN"

(write your answer)

HOLD ON TO THE MEMORIES, THEY WILL HOLD ON TO YOU

FLUSH WITH THE CURRENCY OF COOL

I HAD THE TIME OF MY LIFE FIGHTING DRAGONS WITH YOU

YOU WOULD BREAK YOUR BACK TO MAKE ME BREAK A SMILE

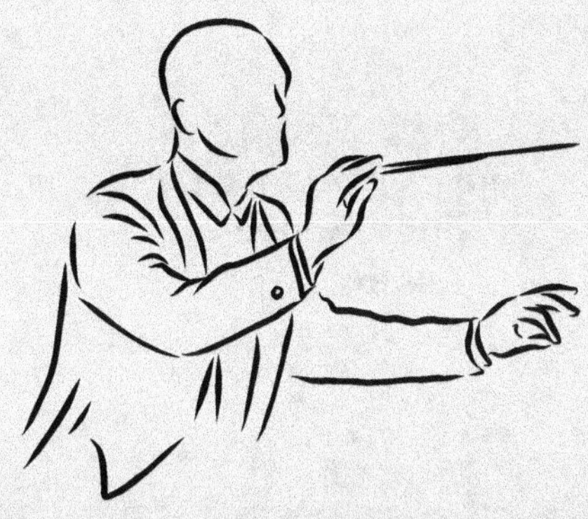

The Albatross
New Year's Day
Suburban Legends
Long Live
Labyrinth

YOU'RE STILL ALL
OVER ME LIKE A
WINE-STAINED DRESS I
CAN'T WEAR
ANYMORE

____
_______________________ *(write your answer)*

____

BUT IT ALWAYS ENDS
UP WITH A TOWN
CAR SPEEDING

____

DID I CLOSE MY FIST
AROUND SOMETHING
DELICATE?

____
____

____
____

HE GOES ABOUT HIS
DAY, FORGETS HE
EVER EVEN HEARD
MY NAME

YOU DREW UP SOME
GOOD FAITH TREATIES

____
____

Clean
The Bolter
coney island
Mr. Perfectly Fine
The Great War

NOW I'VE READ ALL OF THE BOOKS BESIDE YOUR BED

____

_______________________________ *(write your answer)*

____

____

YOU KNOW THAT YOU'LL ALWAYS KNOW ME

I'M RIGHT WHERE YOU LEFT ME

____

____

____

____

THE ROAD GETS HARD AND YOU GET LOST WHEN YOU'RE LED BY BLIND FAITH

NEVER BE SO KIND, YOU FORGET TO BE CLEVER

____

____

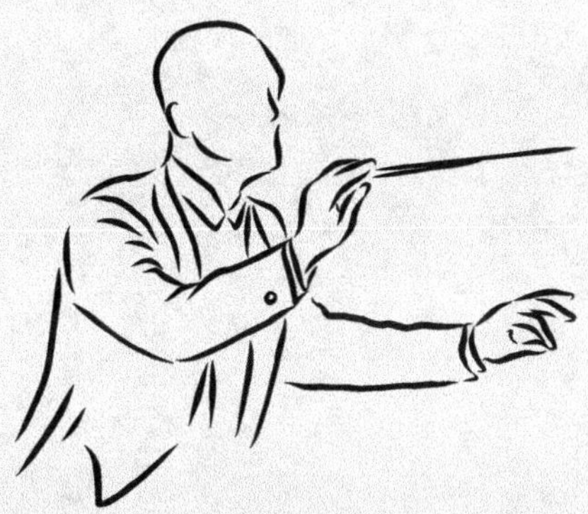

Paper Rings
dorothea
right where you left me
False God
marjorie

AND THERE ARE NO
RULES WHEN YOU
SHOW UP HERE

____
____
(write your answer)

____
____

ROMANCE IS NOT
DEAD IF YOU KEEP IT
JUST YOURS

LIVED IN THE SHADE
YOU WERE THROWING
'TIL ALL OF MY
SUNSHINE WAS GONE

____
____

____
____

I ALWAYS FELT I
MUST LOOK BETTER
IN THE REAR VIEW

YOU HELD ON TIGHT
TO ME, 'CAUSE
NOTHING'S AS IT
SEEMS

____
____

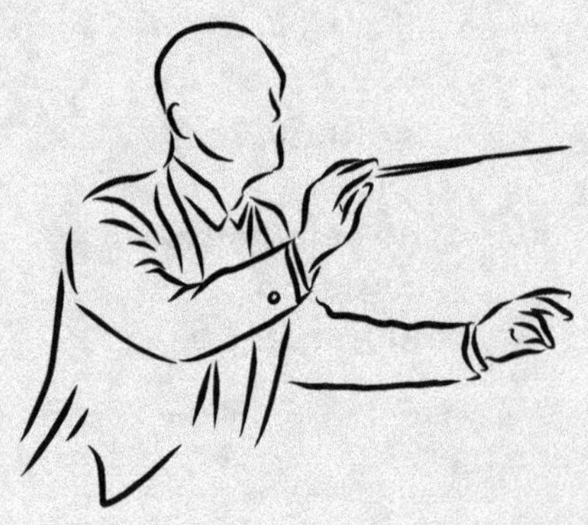

Wonderland
long story short
I Forgot That You Existed
Paris
This Is Why We Can't Have Nice Things

BUT WE WERE IN SCREAMING COLOR

____

____

____

____

CUT ME INTO PIECES GOLD CAGE, HOSTAGE TO MY FEELINGS

I WAS DANCING AROUND, DANCING AROUND IT

____

____

____

____

I KNEW THERE WAS NO ONE IN THE WORLD WHO COULD TAKE IT

THE GIRL IN THE DRESS CRIED THE WHOLE WAY HOME

____

____

Out Of The Woods
So It Goes...
High Infidelity
Dancing With Our Hands Tied
Dear John

DESPERATE PEOPLE
FIND FAITH, SO NOW I
PRAY TO JESUS TOO

(write your answer)

HONEY, LIFE IS JUST
A CLASSROOM

LOST MY GLOVES,
YOU GIVE ME ONE

WE HAD THIS BIG
WIDE CITY ALL TO
OURSELVES

I JUST WANNA FEEL
OKAY AGAIN

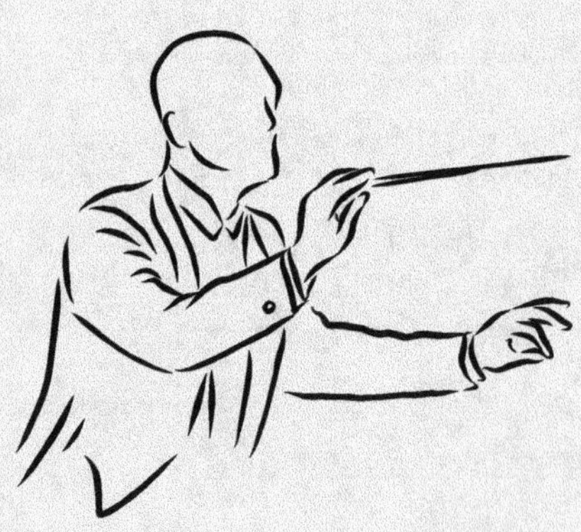

Soon You'll Get Better
New Romantics
It's Nice To Have A Friend
Holy Ground
Mean

**WHEN I FELL HARD,
YOU TOOK A STEP
BACK WITHOUT ME**

____
__________________________ *(write your answer)*

____
____

**I USED TO KNOW MY
PLACE WAS THE
SPOT NEXT TO YOU**

**I JUST WANNA
KNOW YOU BETTER**

____
____

____
____

**YOU LEARN MY
SECRETS AND YOU
FIGURE OUT WHY I'M
GUARDED**

**SHE HAD TO KNOW
THE PAIN WAS
BEATING ON ME LIKE
A DRUM**

____
____

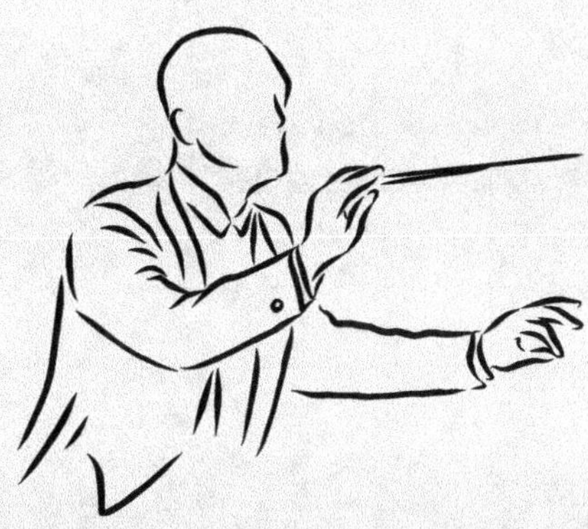

I Knew You Were Trouble
The Story Of Us
Everything Has Changed
Mine
Better Than Revenge

IT'S ESSENTIAL TO ME THAT YOU LOVE ME MORE THAN WISHING, LONGING

____
_______________________________ *(write your answer)*

____
____

EVERYBODY HERE WANTED SOMETHIN' MORE, SEARCHIN' FOR A SOUND WE HADN'T HEARD BEFORE

LOVING HIM IS LIKE TRYING TO CHANGE YOUR MIND ONCE

____
____

____
____

WHY'D YOU HAVE TO GO AND LOCK ME OUT WHEN I LET YOU IN?

SHE HAD TO KNOW THE PAIN WAS BEATING ON ME LIKE A DRUM

____
____

Need
Welcome to New York
Red
All You Had To Do Was Stay
I Wish You Would

YOU'RE JUST SO COOL, RUN YOUR HANDS THROUGH YOUR HAIR

____
____
(write your answer)

____
____

OUR SONG IS THE WAY YOU LAUGH

IT TURNS OUT FREEDOM AIN'T NOTHING BUT MISSIN' YOU

____
____

____
____

I HATE THAT STUPID OLD PICKUP TRUCK YOU NEVER LET ME DRIVE

YOU COULD BE THE ONE THAT I LOVE

____
____

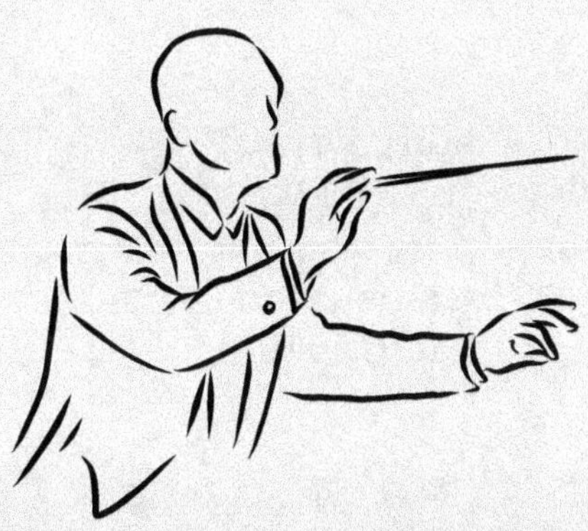

Fearless
Our Song
Back to December
Picture to Burn
Message In A Bottle

WHEN YOU THINK HAPPINESS I HOPE YOU THINK THAT LITTLE BLACK DRESS

____

____

____

____

TRAINED TO GET ALONG, FOREVER GOING WITH THE FLOW, BUT YOU'RE FRICTION

I CAN'T EVEN SEE ANYONE WHEN HE'S WITH ME

____

____

____

____

HE RESPECTS MY SPACE AND NEVER MAKES ME WAIT

THIS IS THE LAST TIME I'M ASKING YOU THIS

____

____

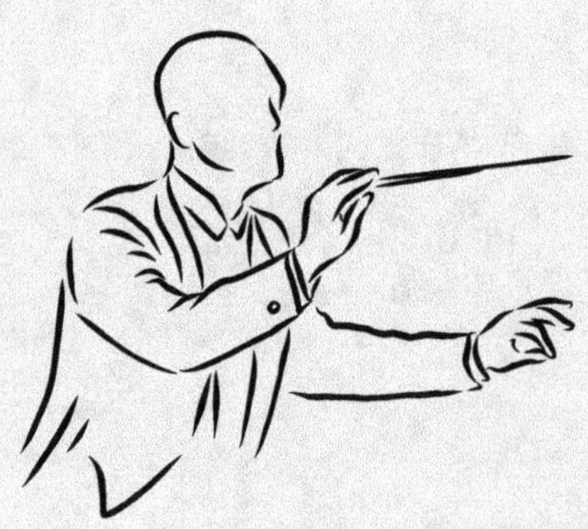

Tim McGraw
Treacherous
Teardrops On My Guitar
The Way I Loved You
The Last Time

BUT WHAT YOU DID WAS JUST AS DARK

____

____
(write your answer)

____

____

I NEVER TRUST A NARCISSIST, BUT THEY LOVE ME

A RED ROSE GREW UP OUT OF ICE FROZEN GROUND WITH NO ONE AROUND TO TWEET IT

____

____

____

____

TIME FLIES, MESSY AS THE MUD ON YOUR TRUCK TIRES

OUTSIDE, THEY'RE PUSH AND SHOVIN' YOU'RE IN THE KITCHEN HUMMIN'

____

____

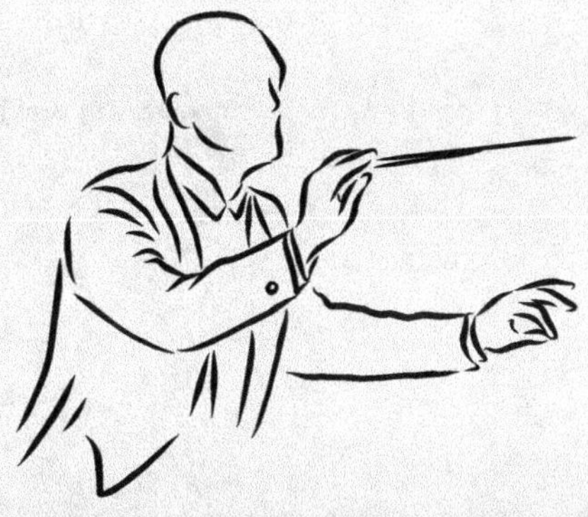

hoax
I Did Something Bad
the lakes
'tis the damn season
Sweet Nothing

ALL AT ONCE, YOU
ARE THE ONE I HAVE
BEEN WAITIN' FOR

____

_______________________________ *(write your answer)*

____

____

SHE IS HERE TO
DESTROY YOU

IT TAKES EVERYTHING
IN ME JUST TO GET
UP EACH DAY

____

____

____

____

A TINY SCREEN'S THE
ONLY PLACE I SEE
YOU NOW

DID YOU THINK I
WOULDN'T HEAR ALL
THE THINGS YOU SAID
ABOUT ME?

____

____

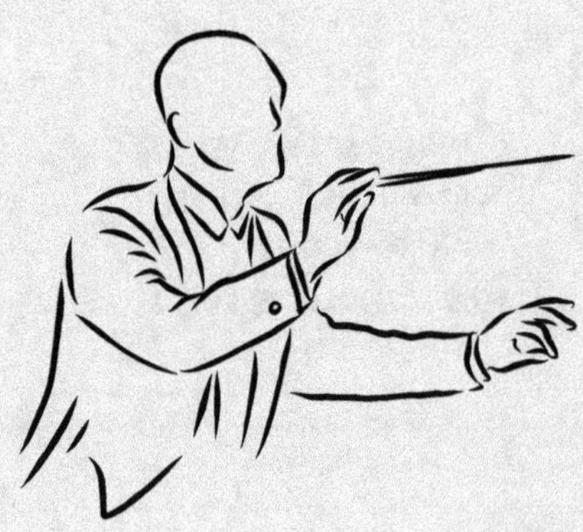

This is Why We Can't Have Nice Things
dorothea
Mr. Perfectly Fine
The Albatross
King of My Heart

HE FEELS LIKE HOME
IF THE SHOE FITS,
WALK IN IT
EVERYWHERE YOU
GO

____

____
(write your answer)

____

____

ARE WE IN THE
CLEAR YET, IN THE
CLEAR YET? GOOD

HEARTBREAK IS THE
NATIONAL ANTHEM,
WE SING IT PROUDLY

____

____

____

____

SOMEDAY, I'LL BE
LIVIN' IN A BIG, OLE
CITY

HE WAS LONG GONE
WHEN HE MET ME
AND I REALIZE THE
JOKE IS ON ME

____

____

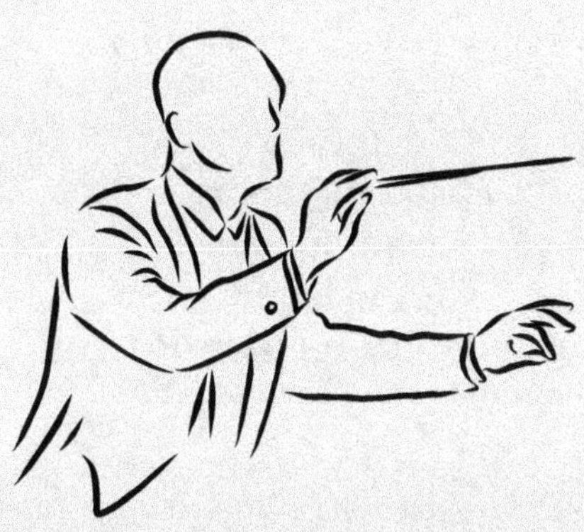

long story short
Out Of The Woods
New Romantics
Mean
I Knew You Were Trouble

AND WHO'S GONNA HOLD YOU LIKE ME?

(write your answer)

I CAN'T FACE REINVENTION I HAVEN'T MET THE NEW ME YET

WHEN YOU ARE YOUNG, THEY ASSUME YOU KNOW NOTHING

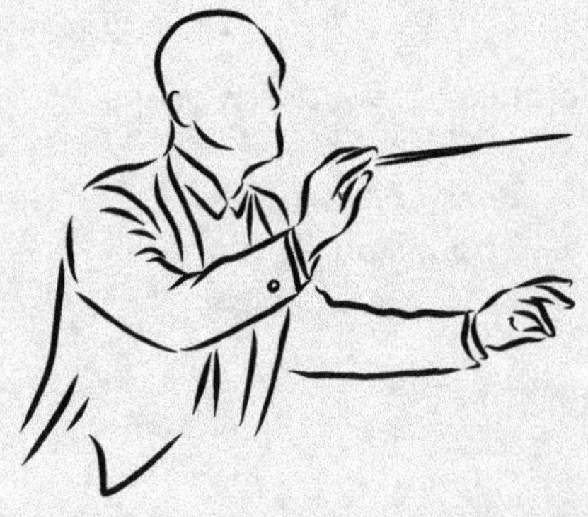

The Tortured Poets Department
Shake It Off
happiness
Don't Blame Me
cardigan

SHE LOOKS AT LIFE LIKE IT'S A PARTY AND SHE'S ON THE LIST

____

______________________ *(write your answer)*

____

____

I WISH WE COULD GO BACK AND REMEMBER WHAT WE WERE FIGHTING FO

IT KEEPS ME AWAKE, THE LOOK ON YOUR FACE THE MOMENT YOU HEARD THE NEWS

____

____

YOU CAN WANT WHO YOU WANT BOYS AND BOYS AND GIRLS AND GIRLS

IF WE LOVED AGAIN, I SWEAR I'D LOVE YOU RIGHT

____

____

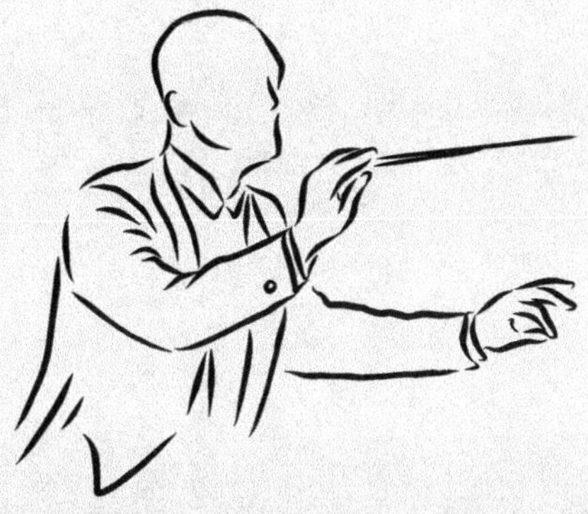

Back to December
Welcome to New York
Only The Young
I Wish You Would
Better Than Revenge

I MAY NEVER OPEN
UP THE WAY I DID
FOR YOU

____

_______________________________   *(write your answer)*

____

MAYBE I DON'T
QUITE KNOW WHAT
TO SAY, BUT I'M HERE
IN YOUR DOORWAY

____

I REMEMBER THINKIN'
I HAD YOU

____

____

____

I MIGHT BE OKAY,
BUT I'M NOT FINE AT
ALL

____

YOU'RE ALL I NEED,
I'M SO THANKFUL FOR
ALL OF THE GIRLS
YOU LOVED BEFORE

____

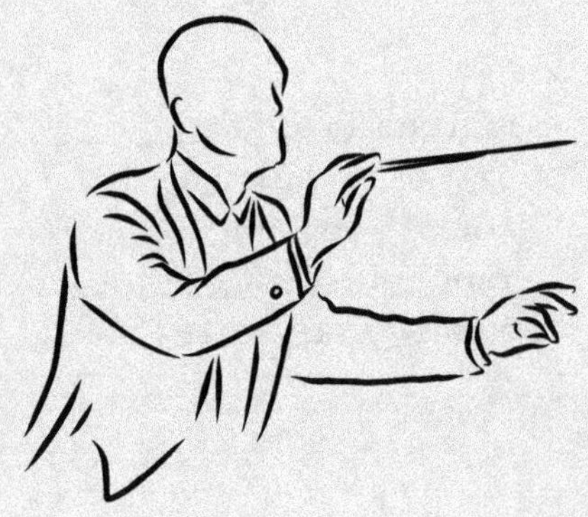

The Black Dog
this is me trying
august
All Too Well
All Of The Girls You Loved Before